This book belongs to

_____

Copyright © 2021 Humor Heals Us. All rights reserved. No part of this book may be reproduced in any form without permission in writing from the publisher. Please send bulk order requests to Humorhealsus@gmail.com Printed and bound in the USA. humorhealsus.com 978-1-63731-182-0

World's
Best ~~Farter~~
Father

By Humor Heals Us

My dad used to wake up early to go to his job.
I knew that no one worked harder.
Even though during the day he was a business man,
At home he was the world's **greatest** farter.

I remember the first time I noticed his talent.
Dad asked me to pull on his finger.
He pointed and I pulled and pulled again.
When **suddenly** out came a real stinker.

One time at the park as we picnicked,
Mom said, "Stop! No more hot dogs!"
But dad just didn't listen,
His butt pooted and sounded like a **frog**.

One time in the car after school,
I told him all about show-and-tell.
A funny noise came from under his seat,
And out came the most awful smell.

Dad always had a way of slipping them out,
From silent to very loud.
His farts were what legends were made of,
And he was always very proud.

I now have two young children of my own.
My father loves to tell them they're cute.
They climb on his lap, in his favorite chair,
And the kids beg him for a toot.

Grandpa's farts are funny,
Even when they kind of smell.
From the teeny, tiny quiet ones
To the **LOOOOOOUD** ones like a big bombshell.

Made in United States
Orlando, FL
05 May 2023

32834626R00020

A KID'S GUIDE TO
FEELING JEALOUS

BY KIRSTY HOLMES

KidHaven
PUBLISHING

Published in 2019 by KidHaven Publishing, an Imprint of Greenhaven Publishing, LLC
353 3rd Avenue, Suite 255, New York, NY 10010

© 2019 Booklife Publishing

This edition is published by arrangement with Booklife Publishing.

All rights reserved. No part of this book may be reproduced in any
form without permission in writing from the publisher, except by a reviewer.

Written by: Kirsty Holmes
Edited by: Holly Duhig
Designed by: Danielle Rippengill

Cataloging-in-Publication Data

Names: Holmes, Kirsty.
Title: Feeling jealous / Kirsty Holmes.
Description: New York : KidHaven Publishing, 2019. | Series: A kid's guide to feelings | Includes glossary and index.
Identifiers: ISBN 9781534526969 (pbk.) | ISBN 9781534526952 (library bound) | ISBN 9781534526976 (6 pack)
Subjects: LCSH: Jealousy in children--Juvenile literature. | Jealousy--Juvenile literature. | Emotions--Juvenile literature.
Classification: LCC BF723.J4 H645 2019 | DDC 155.4'1248--dc23

Image Credits: All images are courtesy of Shutterstock.com, unless otherwise specified.
With thanks to Getty Images, Thinkstock Photo and iStockphoto. Front Cover – MarinaMay,
yayasya, jirawat phueksriphan, Piotr Urakau, Oksana Kuzmina, Ilike, KK Tan, Asier Romero,
Polupoltinov. Images used on every page – MarinaMay, yayasya, Piotr Urakau. 2 – Tomacco.
5&6 – eatcute, Frame Studio. 7 – Tomacco. 8 – ilikestudio, Creativa Images, Africa Studio,
chairoij. 9 – Veronica Louro, Julia Kuznetsova, Giulio_Fornasar. 11 – KK Tan, Noam Armonn,
naluwan. 12 – Oksana Kuzmina, Ganna Vasylenko. 12&13 – coreder, GoodStudio.
14 – Anna Frajtova, eatcute, tupomi. 15 – Danylo Staroshchuk, vesna cvorovic, Polupoltinov,
Asier Romero. 16 – pio3, imdproduction. 17 – Africa Studio. 18 – 3445128471, Firma V.
19 – Tomacco. 21 – naluwan, Evellean, Ana Blazic Pavlovic. 22&23 – eatcute, Frame Studio.
Printed in the United States of America

CPSIA compliance information: Batch # BS18KL: For further information contact Greenhaven Publishing LLC, New York, New York at 1-844-317-7404.

CONTENTS

Words that look like **this** can be found in the glossary on page 24.

INTRODUCING...

CAN'T-WAIT-A GATOR | THE LONE FURBALL | SHRINKING VIOLET | RAGING RACCOON | CAPTAIN CHEERFUL | DR. GLOOM | GREEN-EYED BUNNY | AGENT AFRAID

AGENTS OF F.E.E.L.S!

FEELING.EVERY.EMOTION.LIKE.SUPERHEROES!

We all have **emotions**, or feelings, all the time. Our feelings are very important. They help us think about the world around us, and know how we want to **react**.

Sometimes, we feel good. Other times, we feel bad.

The Green-Eyed Bunny doesn't want his toy anymore.

Let's find out more…

HOW DO WE FEEL WHEN WE'RE JEALOUS?

You might feel sick in your belly…

… you might feel angry with another person…

… you might feel **tense** …

… or you might want to cry.

8

You might feel like you want to grab the thing you want…

…or you might not want to share your things…

…or you might want to clench your fists.

9

HOW DO WE LOOK WHEN WE'RE JEALOUS?

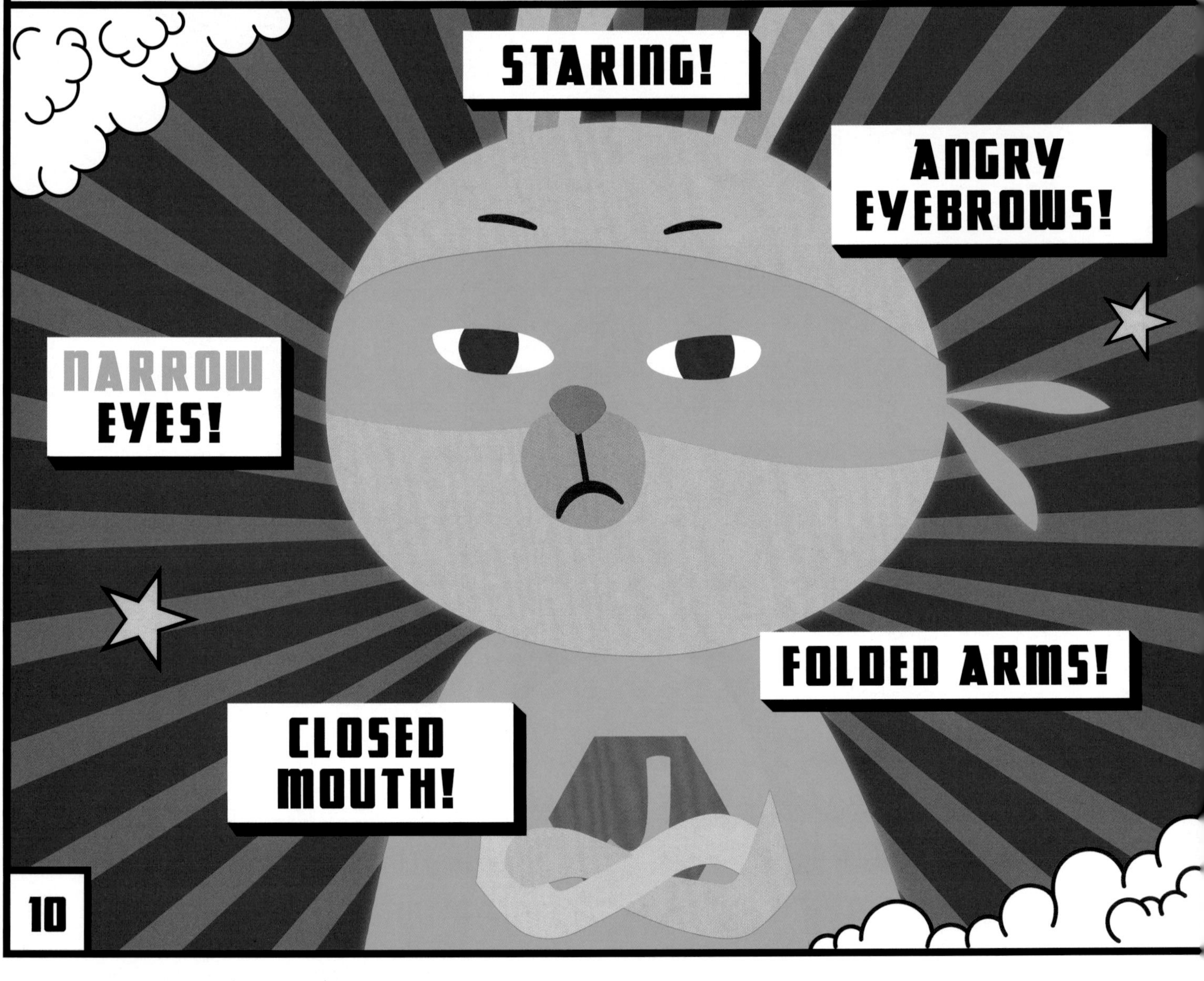

WHY DO WE FEEL JEALOUS?

FEELING JEALOUS IS AN IMPORTANT EMOTION.

Human beings once had to **hunt** and gather their food.

Some people were better than others.

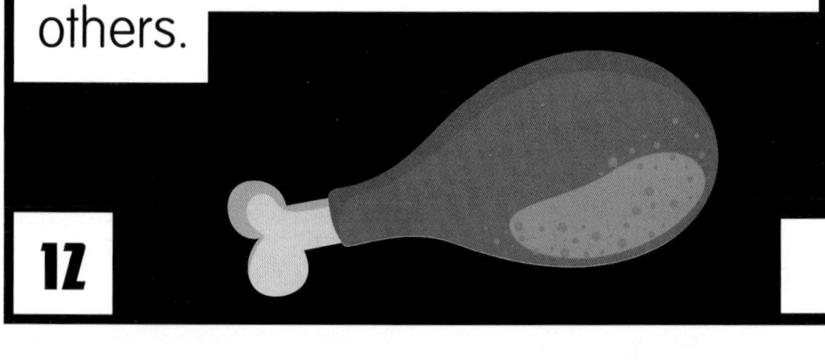

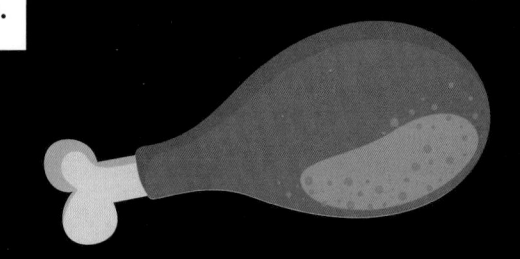

mmm!

WANT!

We **evolved** to want what they had.

THINGS THAT MAKE US JEALOUS

A NEW BABY!

OUR FRIENDS!

TOYS!

You might feel jealous if someone else is **talented**…

…or if you think they are better than you at something.

Feeling jealous can make us want to be mean to others.

WHEN FEELING JEALOUS IS GOOD

Feeling jealous can be a good thing. If you feel jealous of someone's **ability**, you might work harder to make sure you can do it, too.

If someone else has a toy you want, you might talk to them to see if you can play, too. When you play together, you learn to share.

WHEN FEELING JEALOUS IS BAD

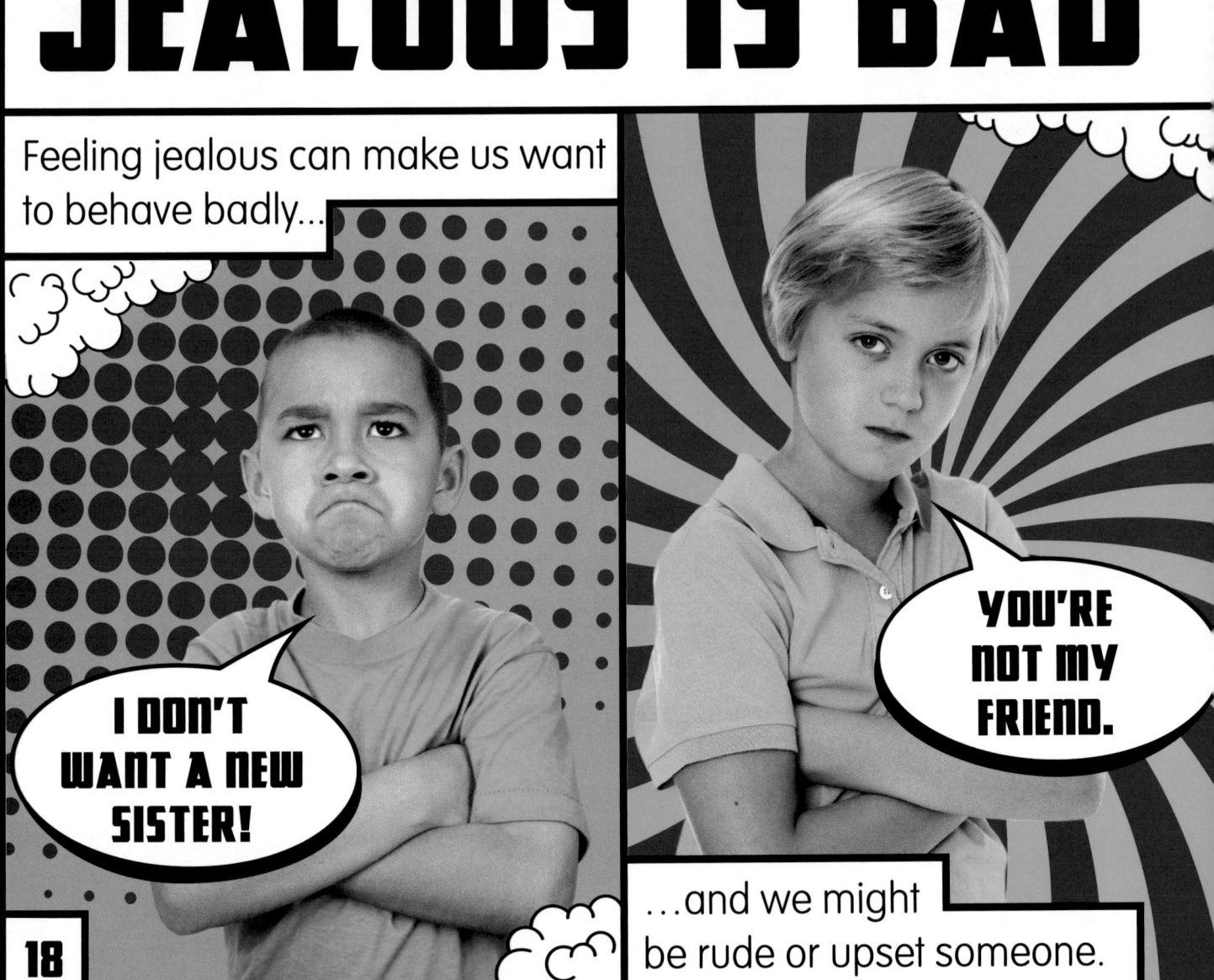

Feeling jealous can make us want to behave badly...

I DON'T WANT A NEW SISTER!

18

YOU'RE NOT MY FRIEND.

...and we might be rude or upset someone.

It's important to know when we should listen to our feelings of being jealous, and when not to let them affect our behavior.

It's not nice to feel jealous all the time. 19

DEALING WITH FEELINGS

The Green–Eyed Bunny needs to learn to share.

His friends will help him to feel better. Agents of F.E.E.L.S: GO!

MAYBE WE CAN ALL PLAY TOGETHER...

...OR SHARE OUR TOYS.

Everyone is **unique**, and we all have things that other people want.

You can get to know new people.

NEW FAMILY!

LET'S HELP!

Explaining your feelings can help you to understand why you feel jealous.

GLOSSARY

ABILITY	a skill or talent
BEHAVIOR	the way a person acts or behaves
EMOTIONS	strong feelings such as joy, hate, sadness, or fear
EVOLVED	developed over a long time
HUNT	to chase and kill wild animals for food or sport
NARROW	not wide; thin and small
REACT	act or respond to something that has been done
TALENTED	having a natural skill or ability
TENSE	anxious or nervous
UNIQUE	the only one of its kind

INDEX